The “Pocke… series of fun educational books for children. The books aim to bring to life the planets in our solar system in an innovative, stimulating and engaging way. My children continue to enjoy the “Pocket Planets” we all hope you do to.

Way up in the dark night sky,

there is a race not like you or I.

Benjamin Bright
Star

They are not green, big or ugly,

they are round and sort of cuddly.

help
errrr!
nip
nip
nip
nip
hello

They are the “Pocket Planets” numbering 1 to 9, from Mickey Mercury to Poppy Pluto all lined up side by side.

Mickey Mercury | Victoria Venus | Emma Earth | Marlon Mars | Joshua Jupiter

Sophie
Saturn

Ursula
Uranus

Nicholas
Neptune

Poppy
Pluto

They live in orbits around Sonia Sun,

and together make up the solar system.

6
Sophie
7
Ursula
9
Poppy
1
Mickey
4
Marlon
2
Victoria
5
Joshua
8
Nicholas
3
Emma

Each planet is different, each one is fun,
a book will follow on each one.

Today they're playing hide and seek,
from behind which object do they peek?

...what fun !.. do you play hide and seek?

THE END

Sonia Sun would like to know;
How many stars you can find within this book?

If you think you know, visit the pocket planets website.